Up The Hollow From Lynchburg

Introduction and descriptive text by Jesse Stuart   Photographs by Joe Clark, HBSS

Up The Hollow From Lynchburg

McGRAW-HILL BOOK COMPANY

New York
St. Louis
San Francisco
Düsseldorf
London
Mexico
Sydney
Toronto

Book Design by Robert L. Mitchell

123456789 RABP 79876

Library of Congress Cataloging in Publication Data

Clark, Joe.
  Up the hollow from Lynchburg.

    1. Moore County, Tenn.—Description and
travel—Views. 2. Jack Daniel Distillery.
I. Clark, Junebug, joint author. II. Stuart,
Jesse, date III. Title.
F443.M83C55   917.68'627   75-15610
ISBN 0-07-062210-8

Books by Joe Clark

Come in and Set a Spell (Poems)

Photojournalism

Detroit—God's Greatest City

Back Home

I Remember

Lynchburg

A Few Grains of Corn from the General Store

Vertical Acres

White Lightnin'

Early American Architecture

Mountain Wedding

Tennessee Hill Folk

Up the Hollow from Lynchburg

Books by Jesse Stuart

Man with a Bull-Tongue Plow

Head O' W-Hollow

Trees of Heaven

Men of the Mountains

Taps for Private Tussie

Mongrel Mettle

Album of Destiny

Foretaste of Glory

Tales from the Plum Grove Hills

The Thread That Runs So True

Hie to the Hunters

Clearing in the Sky

Kentucky Is My Land

The Good Spirit of Laurel Ridge

The Year of My Rebirth

Plowshare in Heaven

God's Oddling

Hold April

A Jesse Stuart Reader

Save Every Lamb

Daughter of the Legend

My Land Has a Voice

Mr. Gallion's School

Come Gentle Spring

Come Back to the Farm

Dawn of Remembered Spring

Beyond Dark Hills

The Land Beyond the River

32 Votes before Breakfast

The World of Jesse Stuart: Selected Poems

Up the Hollow from Lynchburg

For Boys and Girls

Penny's Worth of Character

The Beatinest Boy

Red Mule

The Rightful Owner

Andy Finds a Way

Old Ben

A Ride with Huey the Engineer

This is Joe Clark, a great photographer, and his son Junebug, who is his able assistant, standing near the outskirts of Lynchburg, Tennessee (population 500). They have been photographing people and places around Lynchburg and "up the hollow"—one of several trips they have made to take pictures here. Joe Clark is a native Tennessean, his hometown being Cumberland Gap (population 300) in Claibourne County.

Tennessee is like Gaul, which was divided into three parts. There are East Tennessee (Joe Clark's home), Middle Tennessee, and West Tennessee. Each one of these could be a separate state.

It was my pleasure to do a foreword for Clark's collection of great pictures, *Tennessee Hill Folk*, published by Vanderbilt University Press. I knew his Claibourne County, for I obtained my college degree at Lincoln Memorial University, only one mile from Cumberland Gap.

Joe Clark is as fine a photographer of the Jack Daniel country—Moore County, Lynchburg and up the Hollow in Middle Tennessee, as he was among his own people in Claibourne County. He can track a picture to its lair as well as a hound dog can track a fox to his den. His photographs are stories in themselves. He *sees* in images of photography. For each one hundred pictures he envisions, he is so discriminating he will discard ninety-nine. The one he saves becomes a finished photograph which is a work of art. It's no wonder Joe and Junebug have had their photographs in almost every one of the major national magazines.

Joe's trademark is the large straw hat he wears winter, summer, spring, and fall.

Introduction

IT'S ALL FAMILY

Joe Clark, a master of his art, has told me in photographs a story of a people who have created a legend.

Here are some of the finest photographs I have ever seen. Photographer Joe Clark is no stranger to the people in his Land of the Legend.

Over a century ago, Jack Daniel, accomplished in his distilling trade, was a full partner with Dan Call, an older man. When he was thirteen he had found Cave Spring where the water flowed at an even temperature: 56 degrees no matter how cold or hot the weather. There was no iron in Cave Spring water. It was here Jack Daniel, in 1866, decided to go into the distilling business on his own. He made a product known as Jack Daniel's Tennessee Sipping Whiskey. It isn't called bourbon whiskey there but it is known as Tennessee whiskey, or, just as Jack Daniel's all over America today. It is this renowned product that has brought visitors from every state in the union and thirteen foreign countries.

Little did Jack Daniel know then and up until his death in 1911 that he had created a product that would become famous in America and in many European countries. He didn't know that after his death tourists would come by carloads and busloads to tour the distillery where his product has been distilled for 109 years.

Jack Daniel was certainly a wise man. He knew he would have to retire someday and he taught his nephew Lem Motlow all the knowledge of distilling his product he had garnered over the years. Lem Motlow took over and his name is on every bottle of this product that is shipped. Then, Lem Motlow passed his knowledge and know-how on to his nephew Lem Tolley. Lem Tolley elected Frank Bobo to carry on the whiskey-making tradition and made sure he got good schooling in the art at the distillery. This is why their product goes on and on and becomes more famous because of its taste.

Moore County, Tennessee, the home of the limestone springs—water without any iron in it—is the smallest county in Tennessee with only 124 square miles and a population 3568 people. If you drive into Lynchburg, county seat and largest town in Moore County, you'll see a roadside sign with only Lynchburg on it. This sign doesn't give the population. The Census says there are 361. Lynchburgians say there are more. There's a courthouse and a jail which are landmarks. The jail is seldom used.

Moore County is where the Tennessee Blue Grass country (most of Moore County is Blue Grass) meets the Cumberland Mountains. This is the finest and most productive grassland in Tennessee and maybe in the whole United States. They grow the finest cattle and have the finest dairy herds.

It is also a hog, mule, and horse producing country. But people from all over the United States and foreign countries don't go to Moore County to see their livestock and their crops in this fertile farmland. They can see fine herds and productive crops in other parts of the United States. They go to little Moore County to visit the place that has produced a renowned distilled product—Jack Daniel, the oldest registered distillery in America. This has made little Moore County the Land of the Legend.

Take a look at these pictures. Here is where pioneer America and modern America live side by side under the same sky, tilling the soil, growing crops, raising cattle, hogs, chickens, goats, mules, horses, and hound dogs. Here is a land settled by Scottish and English pioneers, for the most part, and their descendants are still here. While a very few move away, still fewer strangers from the outside move in. They still carry on their traditional music, song, and dance.

Their ways of living have been handed down with only modest bows to modern ways, as Jack Daniel's Distillery has been handed down to men with know-how and know-all. They are people, as these great photographs will indicate, slow to tear down an old barn, corncrib, smokehouse, or even a house when they build new ones! Here the people live well. In addition to working, as so many do, for the Jack Daniel's Distillery, they raise and grow their own food and livestock. They are a self-sufficient people thanks to their willingness to work in this bountiful land with the good water, with the clean Tennessee air that blows among their red cedars and oaks and over their pasture lands.

I doubt there is a distillery in America except Jack Daniel where a chemist isn't employed. They say there they make their product by instinct. Each of the men who have been in charge—founder Jack Daniel, Lem Motlow, Lem Tolley, and now Frank Bobo—has been worth a hundred chemists. Then, they have a taster for each barrel who tastes but doesn't drink. He knows whether the product

has the taste or not. If it doesn't, it is poured back into the charcoal mellowing house and let seep slowly through again.

This distillery is family. The women of Lynchburg and surrounding areas come in and bottle Jack Daniel from the barrels. It is said on these bottling days there's no more gossip left in Moore County. There isn't anything kept a secret except the instincts of the men who make this product.

The men who make the charcoal through which this product must pass to give it taste cut only hard maples on the high hilltops when the sap is down in the trees. They cut and rick this wood. They burn it out in the open, not like in the days when they burned cordwood to make charcoal to use in the iron furnaces here. They formerly covered the cords of wood with dirt to contain the flame. *This* charcoal is made from an open fire. Men who see this shake their heads when the fire dies down to a deep bed of charcoal which is cracked to pea size in a machine. Is this done by instinct, too? Who knows? It gives their product a taste that has won its honors in America, England, and twice in Belgium.

They don't have any written formulas to go by at the Jack Daniel's Distillery. It's all family. It's handed down from generation to generation. And they say a Tennessee man who is trained there will be responsible for making Jack Daniel as long as it is made.

They have a trained buyer of their corn who will not buy any but the very best. When I saw his picture, I said: "If I had an industry, here is a man I'd like to employ." Later I learned he was their grain buyer. The men employed here all know one another. They never rush at their work unless there's an emergency. If there is an emergency, they are on top of it in a hurry. They are all a part of this distilling operation because their ancestors have worked here for generations. They are not outsiders looking in, but they are insiders looking out to the world about them, proud of their product and their achievements.

In these fine photographs you will see young and old at work and at play in this land of descendants of pioneers, this land they have made legendary in America. You'll see their homes, streets, barns, gardens, herds, flocks—and you will see a young teenager sitting on a stone fence, a broad durable one—built by Tennessee hands. He knows where he's come from and he has a future mapped out before him. He doesn't have all the answers but he knows where he's going.

Since the family is the strong unit in Moore County, some of the family units photographed by Joe and Junebug have fascinated me. Here is Buck Solomon (I like his name), his wife Bessie, and their five children. Here are Annie Ruth and Jack Batemen, who says he's had happiness since she came into his life.

A washtub on the smokehouse wall is a reminder of things past. The last time I ever saw a woman over a washboard washing clothes was when I was riding a bus up Mount Vesuvius in Italy, eight years ago. Thanks to Joe Clark for finding an old double-bitted ax by a chopblock in a chipyard. It brings back to me memories of cutting stove wood and fire wood. And, of course, to see a boy in tattered overalls brings back memories, too. I loved being a boy and wish that I could be again. I cannot understand a boy who would rather be a girl!

Here is the greatest of all early plows, the bull-tongue plow. I must say my first big book was *Man with a Bull-Tongue Plow*. I've helped my father make them. I plowed with one from young manhood to maturity.

And to see a man milking his cow while his wife looks on is a good picture. Yes, with milk buckets all around. Many a morning and many an evening my mother and I milked eighteen cows. I love this picture.

There isn't any wonder that thousands come from everywhere to visit this Land of the Legend. Joe Clark has caught the life and spirit of people to whom he is akin.

The people fascinate me. Where and in what section of America living today are there solid and distinctive folks like these? They are intelligent and resourceful. I can't believe they'll ever have a breadline, no matter what is to come in our country.

Here are people who have for two centuries produced their own music, song and dance, their own entertainment. Here are Americans who cling to their old way of substantial life and living, who are fortunate to have their good soil and excellent water.

Here are a people with deep roots in Tennessee marching straight into the future with confidence. They tell their story in these pictures. They will keep their family ties and their friendliness with others outside their world.

I was deeded one square foot of ground down in Moore County a good long time ago. I'd like to get back down there soon to look at my property and visit with some of these fine people.

Jesse Stuart

Here is a great picture, where four good men get together. These men, descended from their old pioneer stock, are as rugged as the rough and beautiful limestone terrain that has nurtured them from birth. Their Tennessee air, water, and foods from their soil have produced these original men with a story written in each face. I'm particularly fond of the man, second from the left, who holds a cigar in his gnarled hand.

12

Here is a lazy photo! It is one of peace and wealth. What youth, middle-aged person or oldster from the inner cores of large American cities—New York, Chicago, San Francisco, Boston, or Atlanta—wouldn't consider it heaven on earth to walk quietly here or stand and watch this herd of Angus cattle ford this stream! How they would like to hear the wind in the leaves. This scene would remind Hoosier poet James Whitcomb Riley, if he were back on earth a man alive, of his famous Brandywine, a stream in Indiana he glorified in poems and songs.

Only in remote rural areas in America can such scenes be found. Tennessee, certainly not the most rural state of America, still retains more of these great photogenic, bygone scenes than any state I know in America. Skillful hands split and laid these rails into this fence—still standing, worming its way beneath these leafy trees!

14

Sometimes a man slows when time is catching up with him, and his once-busy hands become engaged in the art of whittling. And when the old men gather they often test their knives and wood (which is often soft red cedar) in Moore County, Tennessee, in their competition of trying to whittle the biggest shavings. This is done on the courthouse yards, in county-seat towns of the rural counties all over America. Why is whittling a favorite pastime of older American men? I've never seen this in any of the many countries of the world where I have visited. I've seen men whittling for a purpose, to make something of wood, but not for a pleasurable pastime.

What a pair of Moore County, Tennessee, hands here whittling with skill, artistry, and beauty—not the straight but the circular shavings. These hands tell a story! Hands are the greatest tools in the world, and the work of these hands, over the decades from youth to the present, is skilled and they move lightly. What is the history of this great pair of hands, photographed indelibly for posterity? Where have they worked? What have they created?

16

Mr. Marshall's kitchen brings back memories of my mother's and father's, Mick and Martha Stuart's kitchen, even if we did live 600 miles away. To see this picture, with stovewood piled high in the woodbox, brings back a nostalgia for the days when I used to cut the stovewood with a double-bitted ax and carried it by armloads to fill the woodbox. Mr. Marshall, sitting straight as a ramrod by his stove, is a picture of peace and contentment. Whether he is aware or not, he's one of the richest men in the world. Men can be rich with or without money. Mr. Marshall is a very rich man.

Mrs. Daniel's face is one in a million! The eyes that look straight at you through her spectacles have seen many pages of American history flow by her from day to day in Moore County, Tennessee. Decades have come and gone until a new century for her is close at hand! In these twilight years what are her dreams, do you wonder, as she looks from the past into the future? Her living and her dreams are bigger than this classic photo. She looks as though she could be material for a very interesting book; *Life Begins at Eighty or Ninety.*

Lee drives home his 150 Holstein cows for morning milking. They grazed and rested last night. Morning mist is over the lush pasture grass. The cows' sacks are heavy with milk. Observe great photography here. Even the milk veins in the cows' udders stand out! These cows are eating grass grown from this limestone land filled with minerals—the same kind of grass that makes the great thoroughbred race horses of Kentucky. These cows drink water from springs, streams, and lakes. This is the place chosen by Jack Daniel, because of the crystal-clear water from the limestone springs, to distill the renowned Jack Daniel's whiskey.

This weathervane arrow is streamlined into the wind pointing the direction it is blowing. High on a hill so people of an earlier day knew what the weather would be. When the weathervane arrow pointed northeast, the hot wind from southwest brought dry weather. When the weathervane arrow pointed south, the moist winds from the north were almost sure to bring rain. This lonely sentinel perched on this post is a symbol of what used to be. There are different ways to find out about approaching weather these days in Moore County, Tennessee.

20

Mrs. Louise Daniel, after her work day, plays hymns and the old songs she has known from childhood on the parlor organ. Here, in a mood for old favorites, she is enjoying flooding memories with the sound of music. Mrs. Daniel and other women around her in Moore County, Tennessee, whose ancestors settled this land, play their own music. This is a part of their lives—after all, Nashville is Music City, U.S.A., only sixty-five miles north—about an hour and a half away on a superior highway.

After Mrs. Louise Daniel (who, many years ago, married a nephew of Jack Daniel) does her home chores and checks up on the two big farms she runs, she turns to her many creativities. Like so many of the pioneer women, she is very versatile with her hands.

Who made the first cornhusk doll, I wonder? At any rate, Mrs. Daniel's cornhusk ladies are fine examples of the art. These would find a ready market in any fashionable place where such items are sold.

22

Here is an example of what the creative hands of a happily married man can do. They can build this beautiful home from the stones gathered from the family's acres in this limestone-rich Moore County, Tennessee. Each stone was placed in this house with loving care, for this is their home, one to love, where they hear Tennessee winds day and night, singing songs through needles on the hands and fingers of the red cedars and the pines that cover the landscape.

What a prize photo! What a face of happiness and strength! And a mouth filled with teeth to make one envy! This man is dressed for work. Maybe this picture was made where he was working. Joe Clark's camera picked up a detail that interests this observer and will surely interest others. On the cuff of his glove is a White Mule. This is the brand name. Now, approximately 600 miles away, White Mule was something more than the name brand of gloves in my youth. It was moonshine whiskey that would lift a man off his feet. Only the strong and physically fit could drink it. Our White Mule would be some contrast to the renowned sour-mash distilled in Moore County, Tennessee.

24

Getting it barreled ready to stay or go!
Charlie Walker works, as you can
see by the printed words on the barrel
heads, preparing whiskey for ship-
ping all over America and to foreign
countries. Barrels are left eight to ten
years to age, and then shipped. This
has been done in Moore County, Tennessee, for nearly two centuries. This
product has brought Jack Daniel visitors and sightseers from all over
America and foreign lands. The right
kind of crystal-clear limestone water
from springs was one of the main
reasons for its choice of what is now
Moore County, Tennessee, for distilla-
tion of this renowned product known
to multi-millions.

This is Charlie Walker's fiddle. Here beside his fiddle is his bow. Here is a great part of his recreation! He plays for family, friends, gatherings, and for the country dances so popular in Tennessee, especially in Moore County. In this fine action photograph you can even see the veins in Charlie's hands working as he plays!

26

Great details, Mister Photographer! You are an artist with your camera. But your camera couldn't penetrate these ancient hard oak planks so I could tell whether or not these hinges were put on with square nails. Square nails were used for nailing clapboards, planks, and hinges in pioneer years. But here are still the curved indentations in these planks made by the old circle saw, powered by the steam-engine sawmills in my boyhood. My father used to work at one. I carried fresh spring water, bucket after bucket, to the sweaty crew! What artists wouldn't give for planks, like these strap hinges adorn, to make frames for their paintings! Here is something we used to take for granted but now has become a rarity.

Can you believe there is a barn like this to photograph with a yard full of flowers so close to Interstate 65 north and south only a few miles west, while a few miles east is busy four-lane 41 from Nashville to Chattanooga? How has this old barn stood a century? I did approximately seven years' college and university work at three institutions of higher learning in Tennessee. Two of these institutions were north of Moore County in Nashville. It was then I visited this Blue Grass section of Tennessee with some of the finest farms in the world. When they built new homes and barns, they let the old ones stand. Today they live on. There are two worlds in Lynchburg: the old and the new.

28

The famous Bull-Tongue Plow! The pioneer of all early plows.

Here is a magnificent picture of one of the few of these great plows that are left. Note the powerful beam usually made of yellow locust wood. Note the open link placed in the lower hole of the clevis to keep the plow from going deep. I used the plow for years on land we sharecropped, and later on land my father owned, and still later on land I owned. I had two strong young mules hitched to the beam. I used to let my mules rest often while I sat on the beam and wrote poems which ended in a collection of 703 poems titled *Man with a Bull-Tongue Plow*. This photograph is my favorite of all in this collection. This is the plow that broke the virgin soil. May the memory of it never fade in the years of progress and civilization yet to come!

What is more contented than a cow lying relaxed on pasture field, on grass, or under a shade tree chewing her "cud" which is the second and better chewing of the grass she has picked. She is at peace with the world! I don't suppose cows ever get heart attacks. They know how to relax.

Irvin "Yodeler" Branon of Moore County in his work clothes. As you can see, bib overall pockets hold most anything you want to put in them. Only the goggles are too bulky to be pocketed. His riches are in his smile, here for all of us to share. I'd like to get acquainted with Irvin Branon.

Across this little bridge to home is the greatest place in America for them. You see in this picture home with a tin roof and a fine old tree. Maybe it's day's end, with father, daughter, and sons going home! But what a picture—one that captures rural home life all over the nation. And what about the stream the bridges span? Where is its source? What body of water does it join, and who are the families living along its banks?

Here is J. T. Thomas who "rolls out the barrels" of that renowned whiskey with the charcoal-special taste to be stored for aging or to be distributed to most parts of America and foreign lands. Could the creator of this product, so many years ago, believe his whiskey would go worldwide? But I wonder, as I see J. T. Thomas doing this, if he has ever heard of the Polka King, Frankie Yankovic, of Cleveland, Ohio, who made "Beer Barrel Polka" a classic of its kind. Legend goes this man picked up his polka players from the streets of Cleveland, not trained in music, same as the fiddlers, and the guitar and mandolin players in Tennessee, yet they gave their polkas to the world as the Tennesseans have given their folk music to the world.

No wonder Joe Clark found a picture here. Look at the good clean limestone water from the springs where the Ayrshire cows plus a couple of Angus come to drink. Look out at the land beyond in this picture. There are low rolling hills, semi-flatlands, and little valleys. This is the Blue Grass land of Tennessee—its best farmland. Moore County is a land of fine cattle, horses, corn, soybeans, and dairy herds.

No woman's liberation
here among fowls.
She follows where her husband
leads. What their dream is we'll never
know. Maybe it is an adventure for
new territory where there will be more
chicken goodies found when they
scratch! Maybe a nest for her.

This leafy paradise with a stream and cool water running over rocks in Moore County, Tennessee, is something that makes me want to explore. It looks like my Cedar Riffles on the Little Sandy River where I used to go and take a little portable phonograph and play everything from Hawaiian records to the classics in my high school and college years.

Here is beautiful Joyce Finney in her garden. Note how fertile it is—a seemingly endless garden in this shallow valley bordered by foothills and pasture land beyond. She is lucky to live here, breathing the clean air that is still or moves as wind across her native land.

When boy meets girl in the springtime and they sit under a leafy oak
looking over a landscape in the
near distance where there is a horse
with a flaxen mane and tail,
I wonder what they talk about?
Here the grasses grow, pasture
winds blow, love words are spoken,
and dreams dreamed.

When springtime comes
to Moore County it isn't anything
unusual for ducks to get excited and
want to travel. In Mulberry Creek
the ducks have stopped for
a little rest and morning break. It isn't
any telling how far they have
come and how far they will go
—maybe to the stream's end. Spring is
their love season. They get
so excited with each other they never
know when to stop moving under
the clouds of green leaves
overhead while they swim on the
crystal clear mumbling, grumbling,
singing waters of the creek.

Lovestones went into this house—stones picked up from adjacent fields. There was love that went into its walls with each stone and into planting and caring for the beautiful garden.

Corn taller than that grown along the Nile River grows in this garden. The husked ear Minnie Lou Cindy is putting into her basket is as big as those grown in Egypt. Look at her height, maybe five feet seven, then observe the green growing stalks of corn behind her. They are more than twice her height!

Log barns throughout America are getting fewer and farther between. I read an article a few years ago where it said there wouldn't be any of the old log houses and barns left standing by the year 2000. If fire doesn't burn the one I'm looking at here, I am sure it will be standing twenty-five years hence. The barn is in use and is apparently sound and well preserved. Moore County has a good many of these fine log structures.

This woman certainly has no regrets
that she's lived, loved, and enjoyed the
land where she was born—Moore
County, Tennessee, with its
rolling hills, shallow valleys,
flatlands, red cedars, giant oaks, lakes,
and little streams.

Don't you rejoice to see a great picture like this? It almost looks like a painting. And don't you feel you'd like to be able to be doing what Irma and Crawford Finney are doing, riding to their herd of over 300 cattle? This is not the old West! This is in the Blue Grass country of Tennessee.

This is "Jimbo" Reese feeding his pet pig—the "runt" Mama had to reject because she couldn't feed it. Mamas are provided with ten, twelve, or fourteen teats. The mama sometimes has one more pig than she can nurse. Each pig has and knows its own teat. So if Mama has fifteen little ones and can only provide for fourteen, the fifteenth is called a "runt" and has to be bottle fed if it is to survive.

This is a very interesting picture for me. I once worked a long day for a man for twenty-five cents. At the end of the day he asked me if I'd rather have the quarter I was to receive, or a runt pig. Being ten years old I took the pig. My mother put a goose quill through a stopper on a bottle for my pig. We kept him on cow's milk. He grew by leaps and bounds and turned out to be one of the finest pets we ever had. I wrote a story about him when I was older.

46

While Jimbo Milton is feeding his pet supper, his father is feeding the oldsters—the shoats and hogs—their evening meal. This picture brings memories. We always kept hogs and it was my job to feed them. Morning, noon, and night when I wasn't in school; morning and night when I was. I had a special delight in feeding them. I liked to watch them eat and switch their little tails as they enjoyed their rations.

This is father and son, "Pa" and Danny Ray, standing in their own front yard. Their setter is striding across their yard behind where they stand by a gnarled blackgum tree. It is in surroundings like these that the seeds of poetry are planted in young and old as they stand, see the beauty all around them, hear the winds talking to the leaves on the branches of trees above their heads.

Here Pa and Danny Ray have come to the pasture to watch their cattle browse. Notice that they use different kinds of transportation but their objective is the same. Their cattle should do well on this pasture where grass is knee-high in spots. It is said there are minerals and ingredients in grasses grown on limestone soil that produce big-boned cattle and rugged, fast, enduring thoroughbred race horses.

50

Jack Bateman is an early riser in his land of plenty. Have you ever seen a happier face? He has his modest herds and flocks, and he has his loving wife, Annie Ruth, who works with and beside him. Their lives will ripen, slowly and sweetly, with the years.

This is Annie Ruth Bateman feeding her chickens. She looks as though she's in love with life—a kind of wealth lots of people would like to share.

52

I like the ring of Buck Solomon's
name. And I like his strong, good,
proud face with contentment
written all over it.

How lucky Buck and Bessie Solomon are! They're proud parents and have every right to be. Two musicians in the family already and maybe more talent coming along to get a band going right here at home.

54

Here's the tub, but where's the washboard? These were standard equipment not so many years ago, but I doubt there are many in use in Moore County these days. The last time I saw a woman bent over a washboard in a tub of water was on my way up to Mount Vesuvius. I was on a bus loaded with tourists. All the Americans turned to look. Incidentally, this tub is certainly hung in the proper place, on a nail on the side of the smokehouse. And this smokehouse has a beautiful wall with perfectly scored and hewed logs and cracks carefully chinked and daubed. I can't help wonder who the man was who built it and who the woman was who, like my own mother and sisters in years gone by bent their backs over the washboard, their faces gathering heat from warm soapy water as they pushed the dirty clothes up and down over the corrugated board.

This looks like my old ax, at a chopblock in the chipyard I used to know.

Just recently a high school student who lived on a farm in Carter County asked me: "Mr. Stuart, I found in one of your books the word 'chipyard.' What is a chipyard?" It's an obsolete word now, but I used to cut stovewood for the kitchen woodstove and firewood for our fireplace in our chipyard. Then I'd take a basket and fill it with chips and splinters to use for kindling to start fires in the morning. Even the ancient Greeks on Crete and Rhodes, 3500 B.C., could have identified with and understood this picture. They created and, for a while, worshipped the double-bitted ax.

Chris Grizzard's picture here is better than ten thousand words written about him—a fine-looking man whose strength and energy are as clear for the world to see as his wide, wonderful smile.

There's something fulfilling about building yourself a springhouse on your own land with rocks from your own acres. In this part of the world there are plenty of gray, flat limestone rocks to be picked up from the fields, rocks that lie well upon each other. In spite of sweat and aching muscles, this man will sleep well when the job is finished, secure in the knowledge the springhouse will stand a long time as a monument to his labor.

58

There are many things for a boy to ride but a billy goat can be the roughest ride of all. Billy goats are very strong and when harnessed can pull fairly large children's wagons. But they are transport animals only when they feel indulgent. Any minute this young rider may get bucked off his pet's back.

If his pet billy goat loves him dearly and if he gives only little pushes or little love-butts, the boy will stand a chance. If his pet enters this contest seriously, I know the outcome! Have you ever had a billy goat take a run-and-go and butt you? If you have, you'll know what I'm talking about!

BOY'S WORLD

60

When I was a boy the moon was brass;
The sun was a golden eye.
My April valley fenced by hills
Was roofed with violet sky.

When I was a boy my nickel bought
All the candy I could eat,
And there was a path to the country store,
I ran on swift bare feet.

And there was a stream I used to wade
Where silver minnows swam;
When I looked in I saw a boy
Who was the man I am.

When I was a boy I had my world
Wherein to grow and dream;
With chores to do to make me strong
So I could swim upstream.

I would not trade that world I knew
For the man's world I am in;
I'd like to be that barefoot boy
Running in the wind!

Most rural people here—young, middle-aged and old—dance. It's part of their heritage. People from Lynchburg and up the hollow among the low hills and high hills come to the dances, which sometimes last all night. I attended these hoedowns in my youth. Many a time we danced until daylight! No one ever seemed to get tired.

In all of Appalachia, people are never too young or too old to dance. Never too short, too tall, too heavy, or too lean. Slippers and shoes strike the dance tunes on the hardwood floors! Only the strictly "religious" do not dance. And even some of them do.

63

Collis Marshall is a quiet man—an excellent listener, I expect. And with his name, Marshall, his ancestors must have been the Scots who helped settle the land where he still lives and works. He has character in his face, a good mind, and a pair of educated hands —the greatest tools on earth.

Four Original Tennessee Faces. There is Bill Gregory on my left in his bibbed overalls, the most comfortable work clothes ever worn by man! I remember with nostalgia the ones I wore when I worked in the steel mills. Roscoe Philpot, number two among these workers, has a smooth face and a broad sense of humor. Raymond Stevenson, third from left, will question people but he is a serious doer! J. Lee Clark, with a nice smile, a few wrinkles, and a positive face, is a reliable man. If I were employing men; I'd take all four!

Here is the innocence of childhood. What a beautiful little girl she is with her small chair beside her! What are her dreams? I once had a daughter like her who had a small chair and dolls, who grew to womanhood, married and has given us two grandsons, is world traveled, and a writer. So I like to speculate as to what beautiful little girls will be when they grow up. I will not be around to find out, but I'd like to know what the future holds for Shanna Bobo.

Little Chris Dye is a young Tennessee boy. In the background are the old frameworks gone back to jungle—ancient boards sawed by steam-powered sawmills. Young Chris is walking in the opposite direction! Is this symbolic? Are the very young of today in Moore County walking away from what has been—or maybe just away from outside toilet facilities to the modernity of indoor plumbing which *I* first knew as a sixteen-year-old Army recruit.

Smokehouse? Catch-all building? Anyway, it's a structure that's stood up to wind and time. What fascinates me is the tree in the yard, more top than body. This is a tree like one on my farm, a white oak, where my father and mother first went to housekeeping. The house is no longer there but there is an indentation in the earth where once was their cellar. I go to the site now and stare and wonder what dreams they had in 1902 when my father was twenty-two and my mother twenty. In later years, when my parents lived where we live now, I used to go as a boy to bring our cow Gypsy from the pasture for my mother to milk. I love the tree in the photograph because it is so much like one that was a part of my youth.

This wonderful photograph preserves, I hope for eternity, what has been. In the old houses where we rented (we were sharecroppers) from my boyhood to young manhood, we lived on hill and creek bottom Appalachian farms in W-Hollow, Greenup County, Kentucky, and we had what we called "outbuildings," very much like this one. A building like this was either a corncrib or a smokehouse. If a corncrib, we had long white and yellow ears of corn to feed livestock and fatten hogs—also, to shell and grind at the mill for our cornbread. If it were a smokehouse, we had shoulders and hams from the hogs we'd killed for our pork for the winter. Inside, we had a small flat form built four feet above the floor on which we had our "middlings," from which we cut our bacon. We had our cans of lard to use for cooking. Six hundred miles away, Tennesseans of Moore County were living much the same way!

A beautiful goat, posing in all of his glory for the camera! It's lucky for Joe Clark the goat was tethered, or he might have gotten a butt in the stomach instead of a picture. Goats cannot be reasoned with or charmed into submissiveness, and their moods are changeable as the wind.

King of his little flock of hens, this proud rooster is leading them to their citadel where they will roost for the night. He will sit, his toes clutched to a pole with a hen on either side up close to him. This is the way it is around the world. Chickens are the most universal things I know. I've been in ninety countries and in eighty-five of these I've seen chickens and heard the cocks crow! The only living thing I know more universal is the human race. So march, you Tennessee rooster, to your citadel of which you must be proud, for it is better than roosting in a tree where you are not protected from the owls.

72

Deserted now this pioneer building stands! Its logs are cedar and oak. It must have been here a century and a half. What else but stone could outlast it? Properly maintained it could make two centuries. These logs were smoothly hewed but as with old people, small cracks and wrinkles have come to them. Still, there is chinking and daubing between the logs to hold back winds and rains. And the window is there to let in the light needed in buildings and in the visions of man. Here is a small monument to things past.

What intrigues me on the door are four wood buttons and a latch. And this makes me wonder what is behind the door. If it were grain, potatoes, or other food supplies, there might be a lock. But with the buttons and latch to secure this door, I'd guess there were cattle or horses or mules who might want to push against the door hard enough so it would swing open and let them out to roam free.

Here is something which will be familiar to millions of rural Americans. An industrious housewife has taken a needle and thread and strung peppers up to dry to season foods for winter use. She probably will string green beans to dry and be cooked in winter the same way. These are called "leather-britches" here.

My mother did this in all the years I could remember. My wife Naomi has strung vegetables this way in all the years of our marriage, but we never thought of them as a picture!

This is Mrs. Chapman, bookkeeper and saleslady at Chapman's General Store, in Moore County, Tennessee. Here you can get buckets, pans, dishes, fence wire, horseshoe nails, meal, shoestrings, spices, groceries. It's like Brysons's General Store in my Greenup County, Kentucky, where tourists are now making pilgrimages from as far away as New York City. My editor has been there and purchased. What is more fun to go to and better equipped to serve rural people's needs than the old general store? Mrs. Chapman is hard at work and probably ordering more to sell to Moore County folks.

Mr. Chapman waits on a customer in Chapman's General Store. The customer is a typical one in a country store. I don't know whether the dog belongs to the merchant or the customer. But when a dog curls his tail over his back like this one, so I've been told by many who know dogs, he is happy.

General stores, as American as baseball and apple pie, refuse to die. They are places where people congregate. They buy bologna, cheese, brown sugar, eat it with crackers, and often wash their food down with a soda pop. Often they sit a while on chairs or boxes and swap stories. I have got many a story in the general store which is a meeting place for good men as well as being a great service to the people.

Herb Fanning and a friend with their lines out in a crystal stream, maybe waiting to catch Tennessee tree fish. Don't think the ancient Greeks had a corner on mythology. Tennessee has myths all its own, except they're called folklore. To catch a "T. T." fish, you climb a tree, shake the fish out, and let him fall into the water and drown. Anyway, that's what Tennesseans tell gullible strangers.

Well, of course the *real* reason you climb trees when you are fishing a Tennessee stream is because the water is so clear that if you get above it a little, you can look down and see where the biggest fish are lurking so you can cast your hook and line to the right spot. If they were biting at all that day, I expect these two men had themselves a fine fish fry when they got home.

Oldsters will remember this piece of farm equipment: a one-horse dragtooth harrow. I don't know where or when I've seen one used in recent years. But here is one in use in Moore County. We used to clear the ground of trees, plow it with a bull-tongue plow pulled by a team of big strong mules. Then we used a dragtooth harrow my father made from four beams of yellow locust wood which he scored and hewed on all four sides. He used railroad spikes for teeth. It is painfully slow and tiresome for one animal or two to pull the dragtooth harrow but it will pull the roots up and pulverize the ground and prepare it for planting. As my father used to say: "When the dragtooth harrow goes over, it makes a field like a lettuce bed."

Here is a farmer laying off rows with a
bull-tongue plow. I would think this
field has been prepared for tobacco
because it has been deeply plowed
and harrowed until the clods are very
tiny. Observe the laid-off furrows are
not straight and true. He is laying them
off with the contour of the slope, which
is a good farming practice. When the
big rains fall, the soil here will not wash
away. This Tennessean in the Jack
Daniel country, though perhaps not
educated to farm, has inherited the
common-sense practices that have
been handed down from his ancestors.
He could teach the Greeks a thing or
two about farming. They plow up and
down some of their more gentle slopes
and their soil has washed away.

Virginia Parks and her friend share a laugh as that good bottled product passes between them on the belt. Like all rural Tennessee counties, Moore produces such "cash crops" as tobacco, soybeans, corn, sweet potatoes, and sorghum molasses, but one of its most productive harvests is thousands of gallons of Jack Daniel's Whiskey.

82

Old or young, when you see a girl like this, you say to yourself a trite two words: "She's beautiful!" There are beautiful young women in ninety countries over the world where I have been and in forty-nine American states, but I believe Tennessee, where I lived for seven years, has more than its share. Look at Lynn Tolley from Moore County. You be the judge!

Meet an artist at work. Artists are everywhere, but this one caught Joe Clark's eye as he was photographing in and around Lynchburg.

Nature lent a helping hand here. She combined with Mrs. Spider to leave her morning dewdrops on the gossamer strands; then the eye of the morning sun peeped over the hill into the hollow to turn the dewdrops to silver.

Lynchburg, with a population of 500 more or less, is in the heart of Moore County—the Jack Daniel country. Joe and Virginia Parks and their three daughters look both happy and prosperous. Even small Lynchburg, county seat of Moore County (smallest of Tennessee's ninety-five counties), has homes the equal of many in the big cities like Nashville, Knoxville, Memphis, and Chattanooga.

Here three good men get together to discuss a problem in the distillery. The barrelhead makes a handy scratch pad for working out the answer. Note the bottle in Joe Parks' left hand. Though his livelihood, and that of the two men with him, depends on the oldest registered distillery in the United States, his choice for thirst quenching on the job is a different beverage.

Much time has passed for Ophelia and Reagor Motlow, as you can see. But they're a jolly and lively-looking pair nevertheless. Reagor is one of the promoters of the legend and has an honored heritage himself. The name "Motlow" appears on every bottle of Jack Daniel that gets sold.

Four old friends and neighbors gather on a porch to reminisce about days spent in Lynchburg, or talk about fishing or maybe plan for tomorrow's golf game. Whatever it is, work doesn't seem to be much on their minds.

Beautiful Donna Solomon, with her dog tucked under her arm, looks startled or as if she were expecting a reprimand from somebody off-camera. Anybody with a scrap of curiosity who sees this will wonder what happened just after the picture was taken.

In a thoughtful and serious mood, Elizabeth Motlow stands near one of the old mill waterwheels used for grinding wheat and corn to flour and meal farther back than anybody can remember. Mills were in operation all over the place when I went to school in Tennessee. I'll say Tennessee had, and still has, as many of these old mills in operation as any state in the union.

Maybe Elizabeth has just walked here to be alone with her dreams. She's an attractive young lady with character in her face.

Ethel and Lem Tolley standing under a favorite shade tree before their big home in Lynchburg. Moore County is where their roots go deep like the yard tree beside them. There are so many things, too many, they can think of to do. There is never time enough, no matter how you look at it, for one to live who loves life and lives it fully from beginning to end.

Sam Scott, a product of the legend and tradition of Jack Daniel country, says a man needs to live close to the ground "so he can have himself some chickens and dogs and do a little hunting and fishing once in a while." The Seventh-day Adventists believe in staying close to the ground, too. The hospitals they build are only one story high.

It's a fine lot of wood Sam Scott has here. Usually for a winter we cut and stack twenty-four ricks, and we burn them all before warm weather comes again.

93

Brown eyes and blue eyes and maybe hazel. Whose are they?

Human faces are beautiful and interesting at all ages, but children's, because they are so open and untarnished, are particularly interesting. Each of these three faces has a story to tell. Each looks out at you with inquisitive eyes and you want to walk up and say, "Hello. Who are you? What will you be when you grow up?"

94

Isn't it something when local men who are customers at Clark's Store can sit down after their day's work in sour-mash land and play a hand of gin rummy or setback? You can't do this in a supermarket. You shop and wheel up to the cash register in congested lines, don't you? Where else do you find a store like this in America today that offers relaxation and fun to the customers? If I lived near Clark's, I'd be a permanent customer.

Tosh's is a pretty unusual hardware store. Can't be too many around the country where you find horse and mule collars and pads for them; horseshoes and horseshoe nails; washtubs and washboards. He has things old fashioned and modern. Oil lamps and electric ones side by side. Where people farm their land, generation after generation, you will still find this kind of hardware store to serve the people living on the land of their ancestors.

96

His motto is: do everything well or don't do it at all! He stands in the shadow of the place where he works. Here's a man of integrity, loyal to his company, a man with character written in his face, as solid and as permanent as the limestone rock in Moore County. What company wouldn't like to have a man like him?

David and Rebecca have come after school to visit Grandpa Henry Owens. They probably walked over the footpath across the hill you see in the center of this photograph. In addition to seeing Grandpa, they probably caught sight, on their way, of a squirrel or a rabbit or a covey of quail or some fat, fleecy clouds overhead. And the memories will last them as long as they live.

Billy goat is lunching on leaves in a choice patch. He is not too particular, however, *what* he eats. If he can't get grass, he will eat the leaves from trees or the barren twigs. If he can't get twigs, he'll gnaw the bark. Billy goat can live and thrive almost anywhere in the world. When I lived in Egypt, the Bedouins herded goats on the desert where I saw only spare, coarse grass. In Bangladesh when I was working there up in Ishurdi, I broke a molar when I struck a bone eating goat meat.

While C. A. Andrews, here with a handle across his shoulder, walks with his son James Andrews, he tells him: "My grandfather worked for Jack Daniel. My father worked for Lem Motlow. I worked for Reagor Motlow, and you, my son, have worked for the Jack Daniel's Distillery for seventeen years!" The loyalties of Lynchburg's people are very strong.

There are doubtless young chickens inside the woven-wire fencing father and son are heading for. The chicks would be an easy meal for hawks or owls or foxes without a shelter like this one to protect them.

Hound dogs are not only hunting
dogs. They make great family pets.
Here, the pack gets plenty of tender
loving care from human friends. Dad
must be a hunter who likes to go to a
hilltop at night and listen to the music
of his barking hounds as
they chase the fox.

This fifty-one-acre farm is on the outskirts of Lynchburg. A forest, so heavy it looks tropical, is closing in on a lush pasture field, dotted with black Angus cattle. This hardy breed originally came from Scotland, as did many of the people's ancestors here.

Here, Joe Clark just happened to come upon Chris Grizzard who is building a pen for his hogs. The posts he is setting are yellow locust and will last for a century. Today many people who have small farms and work at some other employment don't raise their own hogs. They buy pork and pork products at the store. Not true of Chris Grizzard, an enterprising man who looks ahead for his family and follows the old way of generations before him.

A graphic illustration of how tobacco is speared (cut). First, stakes, spaced along the rows, are driven into the ground with a wooden mallet. The tobacco stalk is cut close to the ground with a tobacco knife. The stalk, with its broad beautiful leaves, is carried over, and jammed down on the spear, which penetrates it. The stalk is shoved down on the tobacco stake. This procedure is continued until the stick is full. We let our tobacco stay on the sticks about three days before hauling the sticks to the barn and putting them up on tier poles.

Running a farm in Moore County is a family project. Everybody helps out and reaps the benefits, too. The boys shown here recently sold their pigs for $1000, their mother told Joe Clark proudly.

When the iris bloom in the spring, Louise Daniel takes visitors through her garden. She has a variety of flowers blooming over a long season, because spring comes early in Southern Tennessee near the Alabama state line.

The ingenious outdoor "hanging basket," made from an old iron tire, a kettle, and trace chains, comes in for a good share of admiration.

"Good fences make
good neighbors," and here
a young man surveys
his world. His countryside
here reminds me of
Kent in Southeastern England.

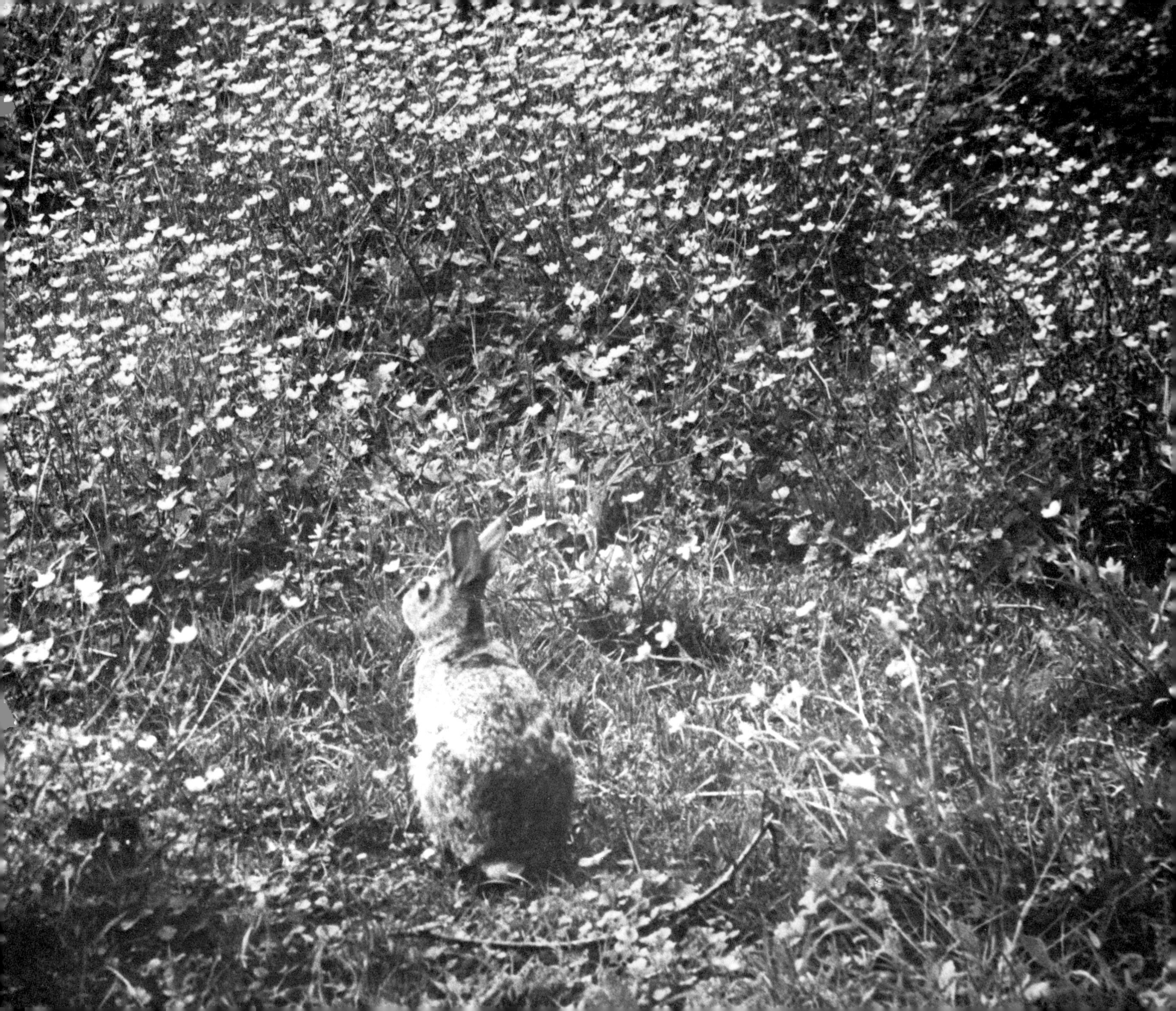

Crawford Rainey beams a happy smile for all the world to see. But he stands back a little to let his wife Maggie have the limelight when it comes to showing the prize tomatoes from their garden.

Who wouldn't be happy to have a home like this in these surroundings? Clearly, Lee Gray and his family, including their dog, are well content.

Hound dog Pete has some special errand to run. What it is he's not telling.

Noontime at Lynchburg Elementary School can hardly come soon enough to please a flock of students who have spent what seems like a long morning in their classrooms. A contest to see who has the biggest biceps makes for some friendly rivalry after lunch.

After sitting so long in school there comes the wonderful break for a game of leapfrog. Boys aren't the only ones who can flex their muscles.

He married Mary Dixie on his birthday, September 8, 1933. Forty-two years later he says of their years together, "Not anything has ever been the same for me since her love came into my life." They were lucky ones to find each other.

Now on a late afternoon as the shadows lengthen across the lawn, he plays the old songs for Mary Dixie. She's heard him play these songs many times before, but she likes to hear them again. This is a land that is filled with music and song which almost seem to be born into the folks who live here.

The well with a windlass was a modern convenience in its day. All the busy housewife had to do was walk out on the porch, drop the bucket down, turn the windlass, and pull up a bucket of cold clear water. She didn't have to bend over and pull it up with a rope by hand. And the pulley and rope were not as effortless as the windlass. To have a well like this a century ago was living high.

We have a well in our yard 155 years old where we draw water to make coffee, tea, and to use for drinking. It's better than the water piped into our house. Water from such a well is earth-filtered, clean, clear, and pure.

Her eyes have seen the glory and the sadness in her Land of the Legend. Now Lucy Sullinger can "sit a spell" and rest if she wants to. Isn't it said after sixty-five you are entitled to be your own man or woman and not have to apologize to anybody? I heard the acting president of a famous Southern college say this one time when he took his Jack Daniel from under his desk at home and prepared himself an evening drink. I never forgot his statement.

This is Cave Spring, one of the many limestone springs in Moore County which provide the water to make Jack Daniel's sour-mash whiskey. The wonderful properties of this special limestone water make it a great drink for man and beast.

Clarence Rollman is a farmer, an adventurer, and more than anything else, a philosopher. "It's gettin' so the Federal government works in strange ways. As soon as the government made Jack Daniel quit making on Sunday, they made the school children quit saying the Lord's Prayer."

When it comes to milking a cow, Evelyn and Chris are at home! When it comes to raising a wonderful garden with roastenear corn seventeen feet high they are at home. When it comes to building their own house from fieldstones picked up from the ground they are at home. A "do-it-yourself" family, for sure.

A rare photo for this day and time. The year of 2000 is just around the corner and here is Fall's Mill grinding flour and meal as they did more than two centuries ago! If this miller isn't pestered by all kinds of people curious to see how the wheels turn, it will be a surprise to me.

128

About Jesse Stuart and Joe Clark

Jesse Stuart, if not blood kin, is a cousin not far removed from the residents of Lynchburg, Tennessee, and thus finds, among people and things, similarities to his own eastern Kentucky hill country. He points these out in his Introduction to, and captions for, photographs which are almost essays in themselves. Joe Clark is part of a family dynasty of photographers of national renown. His son Junebug has contributed many of the photographs in this collecton. His wife Bernice is also a top hand with a camera. Magazines, newspapers, and books`have featured their work. Joe Clark was born in Tennessee and so has more than a nodding acquaintance with the people and places he photographed for *Up the Hollow from Lynchburg*.